POISONED WETLANDS

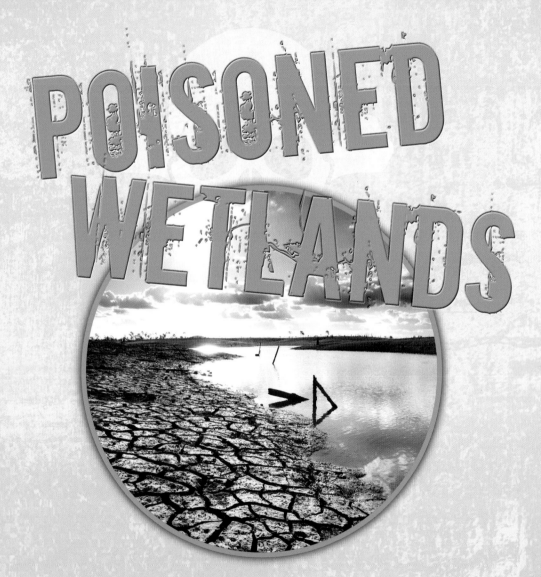

Honor Head

Gareth Stevens
PUBLISHING

Please visit our website, **www.garethstevens.com**.
For a free color catalog of all our high-quality books,
call toll free 1-800-542-2595 or fax 1-877-542-2596.

Cataloging-in-Publication Data

Names: Head, Honor.
Title: Poisoned wetlands / Honor Head.
Description: New York : Gareth Stevens Publishing, 2019. | Series: Totally toxic
| Includes glossary and index.
Identifiers: ISBN 9781538234976 (pbk.) | ISBN 9781538234983 (library bound)
Subjects: LCSH: Wetlands--Juvenile literature. | Wetland ecology--Juvenile literature.
| Wetland conservation--Juvenile literature.
Classification: LCC QH541.5.M3 H43 2019 | DDC 577.68--dc23

First Edition

Published in 2019 by
Gareth Stevens Publishing
111 East 14th Street, Suite 349
New York, NY 10003

© 2019 Gareth Stevens Publishing

Produced for Gareth Stevens by Calcium
Editors: Sarah Eason and Honor Head
Designers: Paul Myerscough and Steve Mead

Photo credits: Cover: Shutterstock: J.D.S.; Inside: Shutterstock: Amazing Aerial:
p. 22b; Arkorn: p. 35t; Drew Barlaam: p. 17; Stephane Bidouze: p. 31; Gerrit Bunt:
p. 6; Orhan Cam: p. 41; Jayne Chapman: p. 40b; DeymosHR: p. 10bl; Cecil Bo Dzwowa:
p. 25t; elroyspelbos: p. 7, 8b, Alex Farias: p. 41tl; greenaperture: p. 14b; Ben Heys:
p. 1; humphery: p.36; Josephine Julian: p. 21; khunkom: p. 29r; Jean Landry: p. 9t;
Kit Leong: p. 13; Wang LiQiang: p. 37; Don Mammoser: p. 34bl; Dudarev Mikhall:
p. 9b; Monkey Business Images: p. 43; MP cz: p. 28l; Ulrich Mueller: p. 39mr; mTaira:
p. 20; NMStock: p. 27; Roberto Tetsuo Okamura: p. 35b; Vlasto Opatovsky: p. 41tr;
Paulo Resende: p. 19t; Salkat Paul: p. 23; phichak: p. 24; Puffin's Pictures: p. 19b;
subin pumsom: p. 38; Mario Saccomano: p. 33t; salajean: p. 15t; Alexey Seafarer:
p. 12; Luke Shelley: p. 18; pongwan sukpoka: p. 42; Matt Tilghman: p. 5; Sergey
Uryadnikov: pp. 30; Krizek Vaclav: p. 11; vagabond54: p. 8t; Arthur Villator:
p. 14t; Hans Wagemaker: p. 26; Bernd Wolter: p. 32; Xabi KLS: p. 16b.

Printed in the United States of America

CPSIA compliance information: Batch #CS18GS.
For further information contact Gareth Stevens, New York, New York, at 1-800-542-2595.

CONTENTS

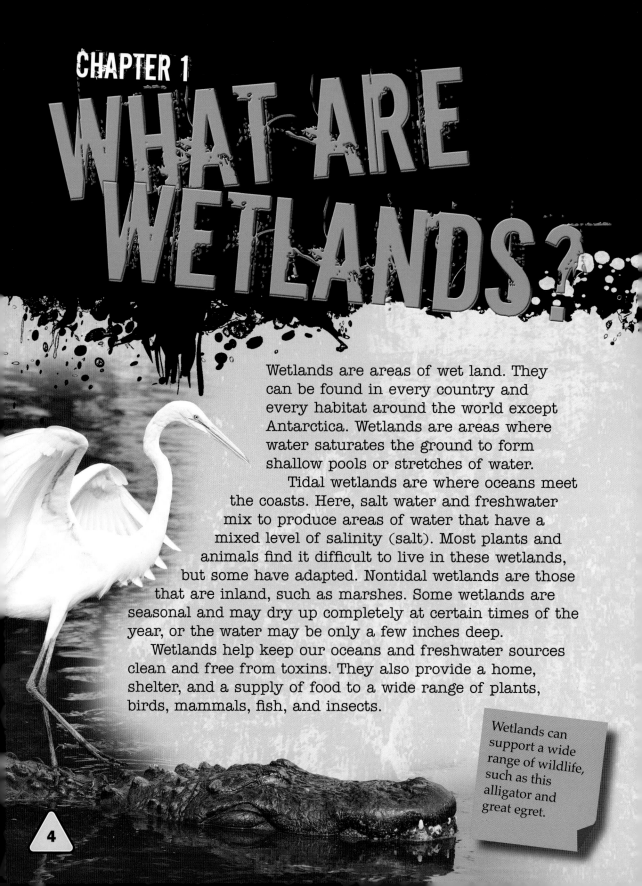

CHAPTER 1
WHAT ARE WETLANDS?

Wetlands are areas of wet land. They can be found in every country and every habitat around the world except Antarctica. Wetlands are areas where water saturates the ground to form shallow pools or stretches of water.

Tidal wetlands are where oceans meet the coasts. Here, salt water and freshwater mix to produce areas of water that have a mixed level of salinity (salt). Most plants and animals find it difficult to live in these wetlands, but some have adapted. Nontidal wetlands are those that are inland, such as marshes. Some wetlands are seasonal and may dry up completely at certain times of the year, or the water may be only a few inches deep.

Wetlands help keep our oceans and freshwater sources clean and free from toxins. They also provide a home, shelter, and a supply of food to a wide range of plants, birds, mammals, fish, and insects.

Wetlands can support a wide range of wildlife, such as this alligator and great egret.

This mangrove forest is a tidal wetland. When the tide is out, the mangrove water drains away.

Wetland Threats

Wetlands around the world are being threatened by a range of human activities. These include mining, sewage disposal, and construction, which produce toxic pollution. The wetlands are also affected when the environment around them changes, for example, after deforestation, when land is cleared for farming, cattle ranching, or construction work, or when a dam is built. The natural balance of a wetland habitat can also be disturbed when a nonnative species is introduced into it, such as a plant, fish, or other animal that is not natural to that particular wetland habitat.

Sedimentation is another serious threat to wetlands. Sediment is the loose clay, soil, sand, and other particles that settle at the bottom of the water in wetlands. The particles are carried to the wetlands by land runoff, rain, snow, and wind. Toxic sediment can also build up in wetlands located in areas around farming, building, and mining.

5

This peatland in Holland, in Europe, is a safe place for this swan to raise her cygnets.

Wetlands Around the World

There is a huge variety of wetlands, including bogs, mangrove forests, swamps, marshes, and streams. Wetlands are classified according to where they are in the world, their plant life, and soil type. The four main types of wetland are peatlands, swamps, fens, and marshes.

Peatlands are wetlands that have a thick, muddy layer of soil called peat. Peatlands make up half of the world's wetlands and are found globally. The peat absorbs heavy rainfall, which protects local communities against flooding. Peatlands also release water slowly throughout the year, providing an ongoing source of clean, fresh water for humans and wildlife. Peatlands around the world are home to thousands of animals and plants, from frogs and newts to the critically endangered orangutan and Sumatran tiger.

Mangroves

Mangrove swamps are usually found in tropical and subtropical areas where it is hot and steamy, such as Africa, Australia, Asia, and the United States. Mangrove swamps in tidal areas are often salty, and the plants and animals that are found here have adapted to living in salt water. The thick roots of the mangrove trees bind soil together to provide protection against bad weather, such as strong winds and floods. Experts claim that a mangrove can reduce the force of a tsunami by up to 90 percent, and yet, around the world these wetlands are being destroyed. Mangroves also protect coral reefs from being damaged by sediment that is washed out to sea from the land.

Fens and Bogs

A fen or bog is a wetland that is usually found in low-lying regions and made up of groundwater and rainwater. The surface of a fen may be covered in plant life, such as grasses, sedges, rushes, shrubs, small trees, and wildflowers. Animals such as moose and deer live here, while otters, herons, and many different fish species are found in the streams and lakes. Fens and bogs are usually low in oxygen, which means that dead animals and plants don't rot down completely.

Fens have soft, soggy soil and areas of shallow water. Many birds nest and shelter in the grasses.

Marshes

A marsh is a wetland that doesn't have any trees. A tidal marsh forms near an ocean, and its water levels change with the ocean tides. Freshwater marshes are found inland and usually form near a river or stream, or where the water table is high. The water table is a place underground, deeper than plant roots, where water is stored in a rocky layer of soil. A marsh is usually a mix of grasses and reeds and is an ideal habitat for water birds such as wild ducks and herons. Marshes are safe places for birds to feed, rest, and breed. Many migrating birds use marshes to feed and rest on their long flights overseas.

The tide is out, so this tidal marsh is drained of water (below). Wading birds such as curlew and snipe use this time to dig in the mud for worms and other food. When the tide is in (above), the marsh is flooded again.

Ecosystems

All wetlands are ecosystems. They contain living and nonliving things that are interrelated. The living things include fish, plants, birds, and animals. The nonliving things are water, sunlight, and soil. The sun and water help plants grow and create a habitat that supports living things.

Food Chains

The health of the habitat is important for the food chain, which is part of the ecosystem. Plants are at the bottom of the chain, whether they are aquatic (water) plants or plants that grow on land. Small organisms and fish feed on the plants in the water. Birds and other animals eat the fish. Alligators might eat birds, and at the top of the food chain, humans might eat alligators.

The food chain relies on the wetland water being clean and free from pollution and deadly toxins. If one link in the food chain becomes contaminated by toxins, the entire chain is then affected, and this can be harmful or even deadly to all the animals in the food chain, including humans.

Wetlands are rich in nutrients and provide important food for many different animals at all levels of the food chain. Fish eat plants and are eaten by herons.

CHAPTER 2

WE NEED WETLANDS

Every day in our homes, schools, hospitals, stores, factories, and offices, we create huge amounts of chemical wastewater and toxic sewage from different activities, such as flushing the toilet, dish washing, bathing, and showering. If sewage and water pipes are old or damaged, some of this wastewater will leak out. It becomes runoff that travels over land or groundwater that seeps into the soil.

Oil that drips from road vehicles and toxic chemicals from farm and yard fertilizers also add to polluted groundwater and runoff. Contaminated wastewater from factories, industry, and building sites also adds to the runoff. All these pollutants can end up seriously contaminating our wetlands, lakes, rivers, and oceans.

In developed countries, we expect to get fresh water from a faucet whenever we need it.

Protective Barrier

Wetlands act as a barrier to the runoff and groundwater pollution that can contaminate our freshwater sources. Wetland plants and soil can break down harmful toxins into less harmful substances. Wetlands also help keep toxic sediment from entering the oceans by absorbing or trapping it before it reaches the water. The soil absorbs tiny particles of pollution and toxins, while tree roots, grasses, and small shrubs along the edges of the wetlands trap other pollution, such as plastic and other trash.

Global Warming

Peat wetlands are crucial to our fight against global warming. Peat is a thick, brown, muddy sludge made up mostly of decomposing organic matter such as fallen leaves, dead plants, wood, and moss. Peat absorbs millions of tons of carbon dioxide from the air. Carbon dioxide is a greenhouse gas. Together with methane and ozone, carbon dioxide acts like a blanket around the earth. When the sun's rays reach Earth, they can't bounce back into space because they are prevented by the thick greenhouse gases. The rays become trapped around the earth, increasing Earth's temperature and causing global warming.

Wetlands, such as this peat wetland, store nearly one-third of the world's total carbon dioxide, even though they cover only 3 percent of the planet.

Absorbing Toxic Gases

Global warming affects weather patterns around the world, causing both droughts and flooding. The rise in temperatures is melting the polar ice caps in the Arctic and Antarctica. This affects wildlife that live there and travel across the ice to hunt, such as polar bears and walruses, and those that breed and raise young, such as seals. Global warming could cause these animals to become extinct in the wild. Scientists predict that within the next 100 years, it could cause fatal flooding and the disappearance of many low-lying islands and coastal cities.

By absorbing carbon dioxide, peat helps reduce global warming or keeps it from happening so fast. But when peatlands are destroyed, the carbon dioxide in the peat is released back into the air, adding to global warming.

Polar bears live in the Arctic, where they swim from ice floe to ice floe in their search for food. If the floes melt or become too small or too far apart, polar bears could become extinct in the wild.

Hollywood Reservoir is a source of freshwater for the residents of Los Angeles, California.

Waterways

In the United States, it is estimated that each person uses between 80 to 100 gallons (300 to 378 liters) of water a day. Wetlands provide most of the world's freshwater by adding to supplies such as lakes, reservoirs, and rivers. Wetlands also help keep our freshwater clean. All water travels downhill either over land (runoff) or underground (groundwater), until it reaches a freshwater source, such as a lake, river, or stream. This water is then processed and piped into our homes and other buildings.

Safe Water

We get our drinking water from sources that can become contaminated by toxic and polluted runoff and groundwater. As this polluted water travels through the wetlands, wetland plants absorb harmful substances into their roots and turn them into less harmful ones. Polluted substances sink into wetland soil, where bacteria and microorganisms break them down, so that they are no longer a threat. Wetlands cannot get rid of all toxic materials, but by filtering polluted water, they can make them less dangerous.

Food for All

More than half of the world eats rice that is grown in wetlands as part of their main diet. Many more wetlands provide fish and shellfish, such as crabs, shrimp, oysters, and clams, that feed over 1 billion people around the world. Wetland plants and seaweed are also harvested and eaten, and leafy plants are a main source of vegetables for communities that live near wetlands.

A Case for Clams

Studies have shown that clams are not just a healthy food source, but they can also help to keep freshwater sources pure. Clams—and other bivalves such as oysters and mussels—filter water in their search for food. As they do this, they absorb toxins into their shells. One experiment put mussels and clams into a tank filled with wastewater. Within 72 hours they had removed up to 80 percent of the contaminants in the water.

Planting and growing rice in wetland paddy fields in India, Southeast Asia, provides employment and the main source of food for a growing population.

Clams living in wetlands can help to keep the water free from toxins.

Precious Water

In arid and semiarid places, where it is hot and dry for most of the year, wetlands appear after sudden, heavy rainfalls. These wetlands don't last all year round, but they retain water long after the rest of the environment has dried up. These seasonal wetlands include rivers, swamps, and lakes. Farmers use them to water cattle, and many migrating birds visit them on their long journeys, to rest and stock up on water and food. Insects, fish, water plants, frogs, and other wildlife also inhabit the wetlands.

In Vietnam, Southeast Asia, local people fish for food in wetlands for their families and also to sell.

WHO'S TO BLAME? THE TOXIC TRUTH

The Nakivubo wetland in Kampala, the capital of Uganda, is disappearing. People are using the wetlands to build houses and grow crops such as yams, sweet potatoes, and sugarcane. The crops mean they can make some money to look after their families. By law, building or farming on the wetland is forbidden, but nobody stops them. Much of the wetland has also been sold to developers who want to build factories on it. Over the years the wetland has been drained and polluted and much of the wildlife has disappeared. Plant life has been badly affected. This means the area now suffers more flooding as there is no vegetation to stop the water. Dirty water has also caused outbreaks of cholera. Who is to blame? The farmers who need a place to live and food to sell and eat? Or official organizations who have failed to look after the wetland properly?

CHAPTER 3
WETLANDS UNDER THREAT

• The Florida Everglades are the largest area of wetlands in the United States. The Everglades environment varies from grassy marshland to murky mangrove forest. These habitats are home to an immense variety of animals, from turtles and dolphins to black bears and the rare Florida panther. However, the Everglades are under constant threat. Over the decades, these wetlands have been drained and built on, until they are now half the size they used to be. They have been fragmented by canals and dams, while pumping stations divert water to coastal towns and cities. Land is being taken for agriculture, and this is poisoning the Everglades and killing wildlife.

The Everglades are a top tourist attraction in Florida, but they must be protected.

Nutrient Overload

Farmers use a toxic mix of fertilizers, pesticides, and herbicides to ensure fast-growing crops. These all contain nutrients such as nitrogen and phosphorous. Add to this the toxic runoff from domestic sewage and local factories, and the result is a deadly mix. This toxic runoff seeps into the wetlands. The phosphorous and nitrogen encourage algae to grow out of control, causing algal blooms, which turn the water a murky green color. Algal blooms keep sunlight from entering the water, which prevents other water plants that are vital to the food chain from growing. The algae block the gills of fish and cause them to suffocate. The toxic algal water is also harmful to humans: it can cause nausea, vomiting, and, in extreme cases, liver failure if swallowed. Contact with the algal bloom can cause skin rashes and redness.

Other Threats

To make sure that their crops grow well, farmers drain the peat soil, removing the water so the soil is exposed to the air and dries out. As a result of this process, the peat slowly breaks down and gradually disappears. Today, only about a third of peat soil remains.

During the 1980s and 1990s, scientists discovered that fish from the Everglades contained high levels of mercury, a dangerously toxic chemical. Contaminated fish can harm wading birds and other animals in the food chain, as well as humans. The public, especially pregnant women, were warned not to eat too much fish to avoid getting sick.

An American white ibis flies over a sheet of algal bloom in the Florida Everglades.

Regular Weather

Global warming could have a catastrophic effect on wetlands around the world. However, the impact will vary depending on the type of wetland. In countries that get little rain, the wetlands could disappear completely. Even if temperatures rise by only a few degrees, the additional heat could cause some wetlands to dry out. These environments rely on regular weather patterns to survive. Any change could also have a disastrous effect on wildlife.

Dead Zones

Wetlands are usually shallow and warm, so they can be safe places for fish and other animals to breed and raise their young away from predators. A report from the World Resources Institute (WRI) states that, ultimately, about 90 percent of ocean fish depend on wetlands as nursery and spawning grounds. When coastal wetlands are destroyed, it can result in "dead zones," areas where no fish or other life can survive. Wetlands provide water for grasses, sedges, trees, and plants; if they dry up, the plants will turn dry and become a serious fire risk in very hot countries, such as Australia.

Water has returned to this parched wetland in Australia. The trees and grasses will slowly revive and grow again.

Pig-nosed turtles (above) and the southern banjo frog (right) have adapted to the changing conditions in seasonal wetlands.

Surviving Dry Periods

Many animals have adapted to seasonal wetlands where the hot weather can completely dry up the wetlands. In some countries, frogs survive dry periods by burrowing into the mud while it is still moist. They shed outer layers of dead skin to form a cocoon around themselves. This hardens and keeps moisture in the frog. The frog stays underground until it rains and the earth becomes wet enough for the frog to dig itself out again.

In Australia's wetlands, pig-nosed turtles lay their eggs in sandbanks during the dry season. The embryos develop inside the eggs but don't hatch until the rains arrive; then they all hatch together. Crabs and other crustaceans have also developed ways to survive in seasonal wetlands, but if the rains don't come at all, they will die.

Defense Against Disaster

Many countries around the world have regular floods. Wetlands can help to control flooding. Peat wetlands, bogs, and marshes absorb water from heavy rainfalls or overflowing rivers. This prevents nearby towns and villages from being flooded. The water seeps into the ground and becomes part of the groundwater system. This water then finds its way into rivers, lakes, and streams, where it adds to freshwater sources and so helps to maintain a good level of fresh water for human use. It also delays droughts in some places.

Tsunamis

Mangrove forests also protect communities against flooding, cyclones, and tsunamis along the coast. The thick, tangled roots of the mangrove trees slow down water that is rushing to the shore. Even if waves are high enough to pass over the roots of the trees, low branches act as a barrier and slow down heavy waves. In 2013, a tsunami in the Indian Ocean left villages shattered, and thousands of people were killed. One town survived because it is surrounded by mangrove forests, which reduced the force of the tsunami.

Tsunamis cause huge amounts of damage to villages and towns. Wetlands help protect coastal areas and lessen the severity of such disasters.

Mudslides

By binding the soil together, the roots of a tree create a protective barrier against mudslides. When huge areas of local forests are felled and heavy rains fall, the mud has nothing to hold it back or break up the flow. After a heavy storm, without anything to stop it, heavy mud slides down hills, gathering speed and causing death and a lot of destruction.

After severe storms or heavy rainfall, towns and villages are often destroyed by mudslides, and roads are completely blocked.

WHO'S TO BLAME? THE TOXIC TRUTH

In 2001, an earthquake shook the area of Santa Tecla in El Salvador, in Central America. This caused a huge landslide that destroyed thousands of buildings and killed hundreds of people. Many rescue workers claim that the reason the landslide was so severe was because forests in the surrounding area had been destroyed for building development. Despite protests and warnings, local people say the government allowed developers to destroy the forests. Was this destruction the fault of the government for allowing so much development or the development companies for not taking more care over what they were doing? Are both to blame? How could the damage have been prevented?

CHAPTER 4

WETLANDS VS. PEOPLE

The city of Andalusia, Spain, is surrounded by coastal marshes that are home to migratory birds.

A wetland is a fragile combination of soil and water. When one or the other is changed, for example, due to road or house construction, weather conditions, or pollution, the future of the whole wetland is threatened, including all the wildlife it supports.

Urbanization and farming are the main threats to wetland survival. People need places to live and work, but building near or on a wetland can damage it forever. In most cases, developers drain wetlands completely so they can build on them. This not only kills the animals and plants that rely on the wetland, but reduces the freshwater available to the local population. Farming also means that huge areas of wetland are drained before crops can be planted.

Sediment Threat

Building work can cause topsoil to wash down into wetlands, polluting them and causing sedimentation. Too much sediment can damage the quality of the water and affect everything in it. The sediment can make the water murky, so that sunlight can't get through to help water plants grow. Sediment also suffocates fish by clogging up their gills, and it kills tiny organisms in the water that are vital to the food chain. Toxic runoff from chemicals and materials used on building sites can also harm wildlife and poison the food chain.

Water Treatment

In some fast-growing cities, sewage water treatment is ignored, or the treatment plants are inadequate for the amount of waste that has to be dealt with. Wastewater from toilet flushing, washing, and cleaning is either not treated properly or flows straight into wetlands, lakes, and rivers. This pollutes drinking water and makes people sick. High-rise apartment buildings push local communities to the outer edges of the city.

In Calcutta, India, high-rise apartment buildings have been built near wetlands, pushing poorer people to live on the edge of the river.

23

Wetlands and Watersheds

Wetlands help keep our water sources pure by filtering water that comes from watersheds. A watershed is an area of land that collects water from rain and snow. The water from the watershed travels underground or overground into streams that might travel into a larger body of water, such as a lake, river, or the ocean. A wetland is a link or connection that joins the watershed and wetlands. Wetlands help clean the water of pollution and toxins before it enters the main freshwater source or the ocean. If a watershed becomes overloaded with pollution or toxins, it not only damages the wetland environment, but it also keeps the wetland from doing its job of cleaning the water. The pollution then gets into streams, lakes, and freshwater supplies used for drinking and other everyday household uses.

This watershed collects water from the surrounding countryside and then carries it to the nearest wetland.

Developers are using the wetland to extend the city of Harare in Uganda, Africa, as it grows to take in more people.

WHO'S TO BLAME? THE TOXIC TRUTH

In Harare, the capital city of Zimbabwe, southern Africa, residents were concerned that their water supplies might be running out due to the destruction of their local wetlands from building work. They claimed that the Environmental Management Agency (EMA) and the Harare City Council were taking advantage of a loophole in the regulations that protect wetlands in order to give permits for building on them.

In 2018, residents accused the city council of illegally allowing developers on the land.

Initially, when confronted by angry residents who threatened legal action, council officials said that they had taken back permission for the construction. One resident said that the council was relying on the residents being too ignorant to know how important the wetlands were to the city.

Why do you think the city officials were selling off the wetland? Why are the residents so angry about the wetland development? What solution could keep both parties happy?

Watering Hole

In East Africa, a small swamp can be found at the beginning of a chain of rivers that link to the Mara River, which is a vital source of water for the famous Maasai Mara and Serengeti national nature reserves. These rivers rely on clean water from the wetlands to provide water for the wide range of wildlife that lives in these reserves. However, today, polluted farming runoff and animal and human waste are threatening the quality of the swamp water. If the swamp cannot absorb enough of the toxins that are flowing into it, they will enter the river system and could become a threat to the animals that need the water to survive.

Wildebeests and zebras gather at the Mara River in East Africa to drink after heavy rain.

Ganges River Wetlands

In India, the Ganges River basin spreads across 11 states and contains more than 120,000 wetlands. At one time, the Ganges River supported hundreds of species of birds, mammals, and fish. Today, the wetlands are badly polluted and filled with deadly toxins. Many of the animal species that were once supported have disappeared, while many others are endangered. Untreated human and animal waste, toxic runoff from mining and industry, and garbage dumping has resulted in these wetlands becoming one of the most toxic and polluted in the world.

Trash Problem

Many wetlands around the world are visited by people as places where they can enjoy water sports, bird-watching, or just walking, relaxing, and admiring nature. But increasingly, wetlands are becoming polluted by trash that people leave lying around, especially plastic. Coastal wetlands are also being polluted by plastic bags blowing into them from beaches, while those near residential areas are polluted by street garbage. This harms wildlife, especially birds that peck at it and water animals, such as turtles, that might mistake plastic and other garbage for food. Trash injures wildlife and prevents them from flying, swimming, or feeding properly. Some plastic also starts to break down in the water, making it toxic. The toxins can get into the food chain and harm wildlife.

A plastic fishing net left in an Australian mangrove forest could get tangled up with birds or other animals. It could injure or kill them.

CHAPTER 5

DISAPPEARING WETLANDS

This factory has been built in the middle of a wetland, so that it can drain its water.

During the last 100 years, about 64 percent of the world's wetlands have disappeared. Today, it is estimated that 1 percent of wetlands is destroyed every year. This is faster than any other ecosystem, including the rainforests. Wetlands around the world are being drained to make way for development, such as housing, industry, farming, and tourist resorts. This destroys the wetlands completely and poisons them. Most factories need a lot of water to make their products. Factories are built on wetlands so they can use wetland water, but this water is being drained away faster than it can be replaced. This leaves the wetland parched and unable to support the plants and wildlife that live there.

Dumping Grounds

The wastewater from industrial processes can be highly toxic, depending on what is being manufactured, but even nontoxic wastewater pollutes the wetland ecosystem. Many industries dump their toxic waste straight into wetlands, or toxic runoff and groundwater is carried to the wetlands over time and builds up. Toxic fumes, dust, and dirt from factories that burn fossil fuels fill the air and fall back to the earth as polluted rain.

WHO'S TO BLAME? THE TOXIC TRUTH

Many of the clothes we buy from major stores come from factories in developing countries in Asia. In Savar, Bangladesh, in Asia, the wetlands and canals have become toxic wastelands. Factories use highly dangerous chemicals in their dyes to color cloth, and clothing factories pour their lethal chemical waste into the local waterways. Also, untreated human sewage is pumped into the water. Pupils at a local school are often overcome by bad smells from the water, and they feel dizzy and sick or faint in class.

It takes 2,600 gallons (9,842 liters) of water to make a pair of jeans.

Nearby rice paddies are filled with toxic water, and fish are dying. The factories produce cheap clothing that is exported to major stores in the United States and Europe. Because the factory owners are so powerful, local officials find it impossible to make them follow the few water safety regulations that are in place.

Some suggest that the factory owners have the support of corrupt government officials. So, who is to blame: consumers who demand cheaper clothing, government officials, or greedy factory owners? Explain how consumers, officials, and factory owners could improve the situation.

Palm Oil Problems

Palm oil is one of the most widely used oils. Palm oil trees grow quickly and are cheap to cultivate. The oil is used in thousands of products—from candles to cosmetics—and it is the main cooking oil used in developing countries because it is cheap. However, this cheap oil comes at the expense of destroying valuable wetlands. Peatlands and rainforest in Malaysia, Indonesia, and Africa are being destroyed to grow palm oil trees. As the peatlands are drained, the peat starts to break down. This releases toxic carbon dioxide into the air, a major source of global warming and climate change. When the peat dries out, it is highly flammable, which means there is an increased risk of fire. Smoke from peat fires fills the air with toxic fumes.

Extinct!

The destruction of peatlands threatens the wildlife that lives there. Orangutans and tigers, as well as hundreds of smaller mammals, birds, and fish, are in danger of becoming extinct or seriously endangered as their habitats disappear. The food chain is broken, leaving animals to starve. Many are driven by desperation to scavenge and hunt in areas populated by people, which leads to human and animal confrontation. People hunt and kill the animals to keep them away from where they live.

This orangutan and her baby rely on the wetlands for food and shelter. Orangutans are close to becoming extinct in the wild.

Shrimp Farms

Mangroves are being destroyed to build shrimp farms. Shrimp farms are destroying mangrove forests in Asia, Latin America, Africa, and the Pacific Islands. In Thailand, more than 60 percent of mangrove forest has been destroyed for shrimp farms. The shrimp are grown in packed ponds that breed disease and quickly become polluted. Antibiotics used to control disease are now polluting waterways around the farms.

The shrimp farms are often abandoned when they become too toxic and polluted, and more mangrove forest is then cut down to build another, short-lived farm. As well as destroying wetland habitats that provide food and shelter for hundreds of animals, the shrimp farms are killing fish that are food sources for the local population. The use of antibiotics means that the local soil and freshwater supplies are polluted with excessive amounts of antibiotics. This could be harmful to humans as well as to wildlife.

Most shrimp farms are poorly regulated. The shrimp are exported to the United States, Europe, Canada, and Japan, where the demand for cheap shrimp is very high.

Peatland Mining

Peat wetlands take thousands of years to develop, so when they are destroyed, it is unlikely that they can be restored. Mining bogs for peat is destroying valuable peatlands around the world as peat becomes big business. Peat is used in farming mushrooms, a fast-growing crop, in garden fertilizer because of its rich nutrients, and as a fuel.

When a peatland is mined, it is drained of its water, and the peat is dug up, made into slabs that can be easily wrapped and transported, and then left to dry out. Mining reduces the water levels around the peatland, destroys the environment, releases toxins into the air, and adds to global warming. As we become more aware of the damage peat mining is doing, there are campaigns underway to find alternatives to peat for mushroom farming. Gardeners are being urged to use peat-free fertilizer. There are also attempts to restore peat wetlands, but some experts are unsure of how successful this could be.

Peat is scooped up, packaged, and sold to mushroom farms, or it may be added to garden and yard fertilizer.

The round-leaved sundew is a carnivorous plant that eats insects, such as this bee. It is one of many species that need the wetlands to survive.

WHO'S TO BLAME? THE TOXIC TRUTH

In 2017, the Ministry of Environment, Forest and Climate Change in India passed a new set of laws that could seriously threaten the future of India's wetlands. Instead of making stronger restrictions on the development of wetlands, the government has said that local councils are responsible for what happens to the wetlands in their state. The new rules have abolished the National Wetlands Authority and have given a new definition of wetlands that excludes up to 81 percent of wetlands, especially vital man-made wetlands.

The new rules restrict the protection available to the remaining wetlands, and now government and local officials can agree to have wetlands turned into giant garbage dumps or drained for building work. Why do you think the government has done this? Why do you think this new ruling could lead to the loss and damage of wetlands in India?

CHAPTER 6

WETLAND WATCH

Roseate spoonbills are among the most spectacular birds found in the Everglades. Their habitat could be threatened by phosphorous.

Along the Florida Everglades, sugarcane and corn farms have grown to feed the increasing population. Phosphorous is a nutrient used in agricultural and garden fertilizer to help crops and plants to grow. Phosphorous is found naturally in low levels in the Everglades, creating a special ecosystem for the plants. However, now high levels of phosphorous from farming, wastewater, and sewage have been carried into the Everglades by groundwater and runoff, creating problems.

Food Chain Failure

The excess of nutrients in the Everglades has encouraged other plants, such as duckweed and cattails, to grow there, and this has upset the balance of the plant species. It has caused several serious outbreaks of toxic algal bloom on the Everglades. Agricultural fertilizer also contains the toxic chemical sulfur, which causes a buildup of mercury in fish. Poisoned fish eaten by other animals affects the whole food chain, including birds, mammals, and even humans who consume the fish.

Water plants are an important part of the wetland ecosystem, but if too many nutrients enter the water, the plants can grow out of control.

Pantanal Pollution

The Pantanal in South America is the world's largest freshwater wetland. High levels of mercury were found in the fur of jaguars in the north and south of the Pantanal. This is an area that has suffered as a result of a lot of gold mining. Mercury is mixed with water and rock or soil to bind with the gold, and the toxic wastewater is thrown away. It then contaminates the food chain. Experts believe that the jaguars shouldn't suffer any illness, but they don't know what the long-term effects may be.

Coastal birds feeding at the Pantanal in South America may be poisoned by eating toxic fish.

Toxic Chemicals

Melbourne in southeast Australia has nearly 700 man-made wetlands that have now evolved into green spaces, parks, and important wildlife reserves, especially for fish and birds. Today, they are nearly all badly polluted with toxic chemicals, such as copper, lead, mercury, and nickel. The lethal pollution has come from decades of toxic waste from industry, some illegally dumped. Intense construction of buildings and roads over the last 30 years has resulted in waste materials being washed into the wetlands from runoff and groundwater. Oil from road vehicles, together with waste from homes and offices, have all contributed to the pollution.

Deadly!

In 2015, a study of Melbourne's wetlands found that 65 were toxic enough to harm fish and plants in the water. Wetland sediment that was tested would be considered hazardous material if it was on land. One lake on the wetlands was a popular place for fishing. In July 2017, it was closed after a fire at a local recycling plant caused millions of gallons of contaminated water to flow into it, but many believe it was badly polluted before this.

Building work along the Poyang wetlands in China has caused severe air and wetland pollution.

China's wetlands are vital for the future of the critically endangered Siberian cranes.

No Place for Cranes

The Poyang wetlands in China are an important winter stopover for migrating birds such as Siberian cranes and Oriental storks. However, these wetlands have become dangerously contaminated from toxic agricultural runoff, discharges from industrial plants and mines, and city waste, including untreated human sewage. The Chinese are now planning to build a dam at the outlet of the Poyang Lake that will threaten the wetlands even more and could cause some bird species to become extinct.

Lead Alert

In the United Kingdom, 100,000 waterbirds, such as swans, ducks, and geese, die each year from lead poisoning from shotgun pellets. A large number of other birds also die. After the guns are fired, the gunshot falls into the water or into sediment, and this is swallowed by birds that mistake it for grit or seeds. The birds only need to swallow three or four to become sick. Lead poisoning can affect humans, especially children and pregnant women who eat the contaminated birds.

The Nile River

The Nile is the world's longest river. It is more than 4,258 miles (6,852 km) long and runs from the lakes of Central Africa to the Mediterranean Sea. Eleven countries depend on the Nile for water for use at home, in industry, and for farming. But this precious resource is being polluted daily by a mix of toxic chemicals and deadly waste. Along its length, the Nile is polluted from several different sources, including agricultural runoff, domestic and industrial wastewater, radioactive waste, oil pollution, and contaminated groundwater. This affects humans and wildlife alike and damages entire ecosystems.

In Egypt, people use the Nile to dump waste, wash, and clean their animals, and factories dump deadly chemicals into it. A report says that in Egypt, about 38 million people drink polluted water. The same report states that people are dying of cancer and kidney failure as a result of water pollution, and they are also suffering from diseases such as cholera, typhoid, and hepatitis.

As these crocodiles glide through toxic algae in the Nile, they can become contaminated. They may then be eaten by local people.

WHO'S TO BLAME? THE TOXIC TRUTH

In Zimbabwe, valuable wetland is being destroyed by building work. By law, construction companies need to conduct an environmental assessment on the damage that may be caused to the wetland before they are given permission to start work by the Environment Management Agency (EMA). However, the construction companies pay privately for assessments that will be in their favor. The EMA is supposed to check the reports, but it says that they trust the assessors to be truthful when they say minimum damage will be done. In addition, the Zimbabwe National Water Authority (ZNWA) and Harare City Council do not work well together, and instead of fighting for the conservation of the wetlands, they are fighting each other.

So, who is to blame for the disappearing wetlands: the EMA for not checking up on the assessments done by construction companies; the construction companies who pay for false reports; or the ZNWA and the local council for not taking more responsibility? Why do you think that the construction companies fake environmental reports? Why doesn't the EMA take a stronger stance against them? Should the government step in?

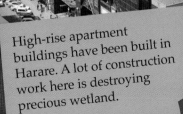

High-rise apartment buildings have been built in Harare. A lot of construction work here is destroying precious wetland.

CHAPTER 7
WETLAND RESTORATION

Wetlands around the world are under threat, but the future is not completely bleak for these precious areas. In many parts of the world, wetland restoration is taking place, with the aim of bringing the wetland back to the condition it was in before it was damaged. As we begin to fully understand the importance of wetlands, more and more environmentalists, governments, and local councils are restoring their polluted wetlands.

Restoration can take time and patience, and successful restoration needs the support of local residents, officials, farmers, and anyone else who has any control over the wetlands, such as governments. Education is also vital to help people realize how important wetlands are to their health and safety.

Wetland restoration can be lengthy and time-consuming, but these polluted habitats can be successfully restored.

Once the right plants begin to grow in this wetland (above), they will attract insects such as this dragonfly (right), which will attract fish and birds.

Making a Start

Restoration begins with soil and water. The soil has to be able to hold water for long periods of time, and there should be a regular supply of water for at least part of the year. Plants that will form the basis of the food chain and are suitable for that particular wetland ecosystem need to be established. Over time, wildlife such as birds and fish can be introduced to the wetland.

A Wetland Success

In Maumelle, Arkansas, urban growth was destroying the forest wetlands—trees were being cut down and the land was being drained. Local planners and officials decided to work together to ensure that the remaining wetlands were looked after, while allowing for the necessary construction needed for the local population. So, the White Oak Bayou Wetland Management Plan was created. They received a grant from the United States Environmental Protection Agency (EPA), which meant they could hire experts who could help them rebuild the wetlands.

The restored wetland has its own website and a monthly newsletter with updates on the management plan and wetland information. There are talks and tours to educate the public about the importance of wetlands, and the University of Central Arkansas is using the restoration program as part of their environmental science course.

Artificial mangrove tree roots are helping to restore this mangrove wetland.

Bringing Back Mangroves

In Guyana, South America, mangrove wetlands were being damaged due to animals grazing on them, hunting, and garbage dumping. The government realized that this important wetland provided protection against floods and storms. So, in 2010, it launched a mangrove restoration project. The overall aim was to protect the coastline against possible sea level rises as a result of global warming and climate change. It is now illegal to cut down mangrove trees anywhere in Guyana. Action is being taken to stabilize the movement of mud in the wetland and so stop mud erosion. The mud helps to support the mangrove trees and absorbs harmful carbon monoxide from the atmosphere—both essential to help protect this low-lying country against sea levels rising.

We All Play a Part

It is vital that governments and local councils around the world have laws and plans to protect wetlands, but each one of us can make a difference every day. Visit your local wetlands, and enjoy them—but respect them, too. Don't leave any trash behind. If you can't find a garbage can, take the trash home with you, and clean up after your dog. If you are fishing, don't leave any equipment behind, especially dangerous things such as hooks, plastic line, and netting, which can injure and kill wildlife.

Don't take shells, pull up flowers, or disturb birds or other creatures. Many local wetlands have volunteer groups that help with cleaning, planting, and just looking after the environment. This can be really fun for the whole family, and it can also be an activity for a group of friends or a way to meet new people.

Be Water Aware

Water supplies are precious, so it is a good idea for everyone to be aware of how much water they use. Small changes help, including taking a shower rather than a bath, turning the faucet off while brushing your teeth, and washing your car using a pail of water rather than a hose.

Be aware of how much water you use. Using a pail instead of a hose to wash the car can save a lot of water.

43

BE AN ECO REPORTER!

- Wetlands need to be managed and looked after, so that they can function properly. What is your local wetland like? Research and report it!

 The Toxic Facts

Choose a wetland that is under threat or being damaged.

- Write a brief description of the wetland. Is it a marsh, peatland, fen, or mangrove wetland?

- Draw a simple map showing where the wetland is and how big it is.

- Investigate what condition the wetland is in. Does it have algal bloom at any time of the year? Are parts of it drained? Have some of its plants or wildlife disappeared, or are they under threat? Compare what the wetland should be like with what it is like now because of human activity and pollution.

- Outline why it is under threat. Is it because of building work or agriculture? Is it being polluted by too much garbage dumping? What other human activity is damaging it?

Report the Toxic Truth

Now, write a report about your findings. Send it to the local authority that is responsible for managing the wetland. This could be a water management office, environmental office, or sometimes both.

• Outline how the wetland has deteriorated. Give some facts and figures to back up your findings. Draw pictures of animals or plants under threat, or send photos of them.

• Explain why it is worth saving or protecting this wetland. Does it supply fresh water to the neighborhood? What lives on it, and why is it important to protect this wildlife? Is the wetland used for recreational purposes, such as sailing, kayaking, or fishing? Why is this important?

• Do you have any ideas about how the wetland can be restored or looked after better? Write an outline of a restoration plan you have.

• If you live near the wetland you have chosen, organize a trip there with your class or family. Does it have a volunteer group that takes care of it? If not, you could start one. Choose a name for your group, and set up a website with a list of your aims. Put a newsletter together explaining these aims. How can you get more people to join your group?

SPREAD THE WORD

Remember, we all have a responsibility to protect our wetlands. Tell your family and friends what you have learned about poisoned wetlands and what they can all do to help protect precious water sources.

GLOSSARY

antibiotics Medicines that help cure infections.

arid Describing a very dry place that gets hardly any rain, so there is very little or no plant life.

contaminated Full of poisons or toxins.

crustaceans Animals with a hard outer cover that usually live in fresh water or the ocean, such as shrimp or crabs.

deforestation When a lot of trees in woods and forests are cut down, leaving open spaces.

developers People who buy land to build on it.

environmentalists People who protect the environment and look after it.

extinct in the wild When an animal or plant no longer exists in the wild but only in captivity, such as zoos.

flammable Easily set on fire.

groundwater Water that has seeped or leaked into the ground.

hazardous Very dangerous, risky or unsafe.

migrating Moving from one country to another; birds on their seasonal journey from one place to another.

nature reserves Protected areas of land where animals and plants can live safely.

nontidal Not affected by the ocean tides.

nutrients Substances that help make sure that living things stay strong and grow in a healthy way.

organisms Living things.

parched Very dry and in need of water.

radioactive Having or making a form of energy called radiation, which can be very dangerous and affect the health of living things.

runoff Water that drains away by running over land and into rivers, lakes, and the ocean.

saturates Makes soggy or wet with water.

sediment Organic matter, such as soil, that sinks to the bottom of water, such as in a lake or stream.

tidal Something that changes with the tides of the ocean.

toxins Harmful poisons that can cause death.

tsunami A huge tidal wave usually caused by an earthquake or other disturbance in the ocean.

urbanization Building developments on the outskirts of a city or town.

watersheds Areas of high land that separate rivers.

FOR MORE INFORMATION

Books

Perdew, Laura. *Bringing Back Our Wetlands* (Conservation Success Stories). Minneapolis, MN: Essential Library, 2018.

Roche, Jess. *Jaw-Dropping Geography: Fun Learning Facts About Wondrous Wetlands.* CreateSpace Independent Publishing Platform, 2015.

Schomp, Virginia. *24 Hours in the Wetlands* (A Day in an Ecosystem). New York, NY: Cavendish Square Publishing, 2013.

Sill, Cathryn. *Wetlands* (About Habitats). Atlanta, GA: Peachtree, 2013.

Websites

kids.nceas.ucsb.edu/biomes/freshwaterwetlands.html
Discover more about the animals and plants that need freshwater wetlands to survive and why wetlands are so important for humans, too.

www.nationalgeographic.org/encyclopedia/wetland
Explore wetlands throughout the United States and around the world.

www.nps.gov/ever/learn/kidsyouth/learning-about-the-everglades.htm
Take a walk around the Everglades, and learn why they are so special and need to be looked after.

www.worldwildlife.org/habitats/wetlands
Learn about what threatens wetlands and what the World Wildlife Fund (WWF) is doing to help.

Publisher's note to educators and parents: Our editors have carefully reviewed these websites to ensure that they are suitable for students. Many websites change frequently, however, and we cannot guarantee that a site's future contents will continue to meet our high standards of quality and educational value. Be advised that students should be closely supervised whenever they access the Internet.

INDEX